W0006958

RIVERBED OF MEMORY

DAISY ZAMORA

Translated from the Spanish by
Barbara Paschke

Pocket Poets Series № 49

CITY LIGHTS
San Francisco

Cover design by Rex Ray
Book design by Amy Scholder
Typography by Harvest Graphics

Library of Congress Cataloging-in-Publication Data

Zamora, Daisy.
    [En limpio se escribe la vida.   English & Spanish]
    Riverbed of memory / by Daisy Zamora ; translated from the
Spanish by Barbara Paschke.
        p.   cm. — (Pocket poets series ;#49)
    ISBN 0-87286-273-9 : $7.95
    I. Paschke, Barbara.   II. Title.
PQ7529.2.Z36A26   1993
861 — dc20   92-34355
                                                               CIP

City Lights Books are available to bookstores through our primary
distributor: Subterranean Company. P. O. Box 160, 265 S. 5th St.,
Monroe, OR 97456. 503-847-5274. Toll-free orders 800-274-7826. FAX
503-847-6018. Our books are also available through library jobbers and
regional distributors. For personal orders and catalogs, please write to
City Lights Books, 261 Columbus Avenue, San Francisco, CA 94133.

CITY LIGHTS BOOKS are edited by Lawrence Ferlinghetti and
Nancy J. Peters and published at the City Lights Bookstore,
261 Columbus Avenue, San Francisco, CA 94133.

TRANSLATOR'S ACKNOWLEDGMENTS

I would like to thank Margot Pepper for her work on translations (indicated after poems by her initials); Maria Elena Gutierrez, Lawrence Ferlinghetti and Alejandro Murguía for helpful suggestions; and Nancy Peters and Amy Scholder at City Lights. Thanks also to Margaret Randall, whose book *Sandino's Daughters* provided valuable background information. Special thanks to David and Galen Volpendesta, my husband and son, for their love and support and trips to the park to leave me time to work. And finally, *gracías* to Daisy Zamora for sharing her life and her poetry with the world.

RIVERBED OR MEMORY

RIVERBED OR MEMORY

INTRODUCTION

Like many Central American writers, Daisy Zamora contends that "A poet must be a witness to her time." She is part of a generation of Nicaraguans that has things to say that no one will ever say again, a generation that remembers what life was like before, during, and after the Nicaraguan Revolution. In these gentle, angry, loving, painful, hopeful, and political poems, she bears witness, plumbing "the riverbed of memory" and in so doing, illuminates her experiences and those of others, particularly other women, so that their stories will not be lost. The poems draw one into a web of intimate sensibilities, grounded in the concrete and even the mundane. Here truly is witness to a time, to a life, to an extraordinary woman's life, and to a revolution.

The diverse themes of the poems — women, motherhood, family, politics, life and death — are rooted in the land and people of Nicaragua, yet are universally recognizable. Daisy paints portraits of women of all classes, writes elegies for beloved family members, and looks back on her childhood, often using her own body as a metaphor and starting point. She interweaves the personal and the political in her poetry as she has in her life, mourning the devastation of war and celebrating those who have played a part in her life. The resulting richness is deeply moving, even more so because of its understatedness, its direct language and crystalline images. On one page, a poem not much more than a fragment:

> Like a little leaf of willow
> > or bamboo
> you stick to me
> looking for my delicate
> > shadow.

In other poems, Daisy is the chronicler of women's lives. Sharp vignettes give us glimpses of working women's lives in Nicaragua, such as the waitress who

> . . . opens the freezer, takes out ice cream,
> stirs milk, opens beers;
> she fixes cocktails, throws bottle caps on the floor,
> puts everything on the counter and serves.
> She looks like the others
> but she's different:
> > she glows
> when her boyfriend peeks
> from behind the glass door
> > of the cafeteria.

Here also are tributes to the women who fought in all ways

in the Revolution, as in "Let me talk about my women"

> Who could fail to mention
> Juana Cruz, Jinotegan bartender,
> exchanging brandy for bullets
> and advising her girl to extract information
> from guards and marines
> . . .
> Who can say a word about her
> and her whores, the cleanest and most dignified
> ever known.

Daisy Zamora was born into a well-to-do, upper-middle-class Nicaraguan family, active in liberal politics. When she was four years old, her father was arrested in an attempted coup against Somoza. When she recognized him in a photograph of prisoners on the front page of the newspaper, she was told by her family that he had gone on a business trip and that the person in the picture only looked like her father. She finally gave up insisting, then suffered from nightmares; she has cited this incident as her first memory of the effect of politics on life. Raised by her grandparents and a great aunt and educated in convent schools, she remembers being a shy child who loved to read and who began writing poetry at an early age. When she arrived at the University in Managua in 1967, her life began to change.

Although she involved herself in political work, she felt unable to commit fully to the revoluntionary movement because of her class background. Moving to Chinandega with her husband, Dionisio, who had taken a job as an engineer in a sugar mill, she became increasingly aware of the social injustice and rigid class system endemic to Nicaragua, and she shocked the community by teaching in a school for worker's children. She and Dionisio became more and more politically active, but still felt unable to devote themselves exclusively to the struggle.

Then in 1972, Daisy returned to Managua to nurse her grandfather, who was dying of cancer. In those last few months of his life, he attempted to persuade her that it was time she take a stand, suggesting that if he were young, he would be in the mountains with the *guerrilla*. For Daisy, the death of her grandfather, who had been the most important person in her life, signified a break with the past, and by 1974 she and Dionisio were immersed in both overt and covert political action in Chinandega. When working there became impossible because of threats from Somoza's Guard, they moved to Managua and were immediately contacted by the Sandinista Party. From 1975 until the triumph in 1979, Daisy Zamora worked for the revolution both behind and on the front lines — she was part of the operation that took over the National Palace. Two poems in this collection — "A Scattered Squad" and "And I Cursed the

Moon" — are personal recollections of the aftermath of that effort. After she fled into exile in Honduras and Costa Rica, she worked as announcer and program director for clandestine Radio Sandino, an important lifeline to supporters of the revolution.

When she returned to Managua in 1979, she continued working in the Sandinista Party and served as Vice-Minister of Culture, director of the North American desk in the Department of International Relations, and head of publishing at a research institute. She is now a professor at Universidad Centroamericana in Manuagua, where she teaches 17th-century literature and a course on Sor Juan de la Cruz. Her most recent book is an anthology of poetry by Nicaraguan women, published in March of 1992.

B.P.

AL PIE DE
LA DIOSA BLANCA

Es cierto que te he traicionado.
Por años te pospuse con argumentos vanos.
¡Cómo desatendí tus llamados!
Quise taparme los oídos con la dorada
cera de las abejas, pero
          no era de sirenas tu canto.
Hasta en sueños me perseguías
e hiciste yunque de mi pobre cabeza
y yo, necia, me negaba a obedecerte.

Pero prevaleciste, oh Diosa, sobre mí
y sobre la voluntad de quienes quisieron
encadenarme en el antiquísimo rol.

Tampoco puede decirse que fui cobarde
porque de algún modo supe resistir.
Te filtrabas, aliento que hinchó el alma.
He sobrevivido al menos, Diosa, y te hablo,
Vencedora: soy tuya para siempre.

AT THE FOOT OF
THE GODDESS

It's true that I have betrayed you.
For years I put you off with empty arguments.
How I ignored your calls!
I wanted to plug my ears with golden
beeswax, but
          your song was not that of a siren.
Even in dreams you pursued me;
you made an anvil of my poor head
and I, stubborn, refused to obey you.

But you, goddess, prevailed over me
and over the will of those who wished
to enchain me in an ancient role.

No one can say I was a coward
because in some way I knew how to resist.
You filtered in, a breath that expanded my soul.
At least I have survived, Goddess, and I speak to you,
Victor: I am yours forever.

PUERTA EN LA MEMORIA

A costumbrada a levantar mis ojos para verlo siempre desde
                                                    abajo
en imponente perspectiva:
                    Sólido mentón,
                    nítido bigote blanco,
maliciosas chispas oscuras que me hacían guiños cariñosos
y en la frente la noble arruga horizontal,
                    la airosa cabeza de plata.

De dónde sacaré fuerzas para enfrentar cada mañana
esa puerta cerrada de mi dormitorio
justo frente al suyo, abierto de par en par
                    desde la madrugada.
El, enfermo, impecable piyama entre las sábanas
                    con punto de almidón,
pañuelo oloroso a lavanda o Jean Marie Fariña Tres Coronas;
el rostro vuelto hacia mi puerta:
Todo él, todo lo que queda de él, montoncito de huesos
                    hacia mi puerta
con la fuerza del desamparo en sus ojos
                    clavados en mi puerta,

DOOR IN MY MEMORY

Accustomed to raising my eyes to see him from below,
always an imposing perspective:
                              Solid chin,
                              clipped white moustache,
malicious dark sparks that winked lovingly at me,
and the aristocratic horizontal crease in the forehead,
                              the elegant silver head.

From where did I gather strength each morning to confront
that closed bedroom door of mine
just opposite his, wide open since dawn.
He, unwell, impeccable pajamas between the sheets
                              with just a pinch of starch,
handkerchief smelling of lavender or of Jean Marie Fariña
                              Tres Coronas;
his face turned toward my door.
All of him, all that was left of him, a small pile of bones
                              toward my door
with the power of helplessness in his eyes
                              nailed to my door,

niño decrépito, agónico, que ha despertado íngrimo
                    por última vez
y busca en los ojos de la nieta, la madre /
                        la mujer.

decrepit child, dying, who has awakened lonely
                              for the last time
and looks into the eyes of his grandaughter, mother /
                                        wife.

QUÉ MANOS A TRAVÉS
DE MIS MANOS

Las anchas manos pecosas y morenas de mi abuelo
con igual destreza vendaban una herida,
cortaban gardenias
o me suspendían en el aire feliz de la infancia.

Las manos de mi abuela paterna
artríticas ya cerca de su muerte,
una vez fueron frágiles manos, filigrana de plata,
argolla de matrimonio en el anular izquierdo;
pitillera y traguito de *scotch* o de vino jerez
en atardeceres de blancas celosías
y pisos de madera olorosos a cera,
recostada en su *chaise-longue* leyendo trágicas historias
de heroínas anémicas o tísicas.

Mi padre siempre cuidó la transparencia de sus manos
delicadas como alas de querube
hechas para lucirlas
con violín o batuta.

Mi madre heredó las manos de mi abuelo Arturo,
pequeñas y nudosas, con dedos romos.

WHAT HANDS THROUGH
MY HANDS

The broad brown freckled hands of my grandfather
with equal dexterity bandaged a wound,
cut gardenias
or swung me around in the happy air of childhood.

The hands of my paternal grandmother
arthritic near death,
were once fragile hands, silver filigree
wedding band on her left ring finger;
a cigarette case, a sip of scotch or sherry
in the dusk of white latticed windows
and wooden floors smelling of wax,
reclining on her *chaise-longue* reading romantic novels
about anemic or consumptive heroines.

My father always took care of the transparency of his hands
delicate as cherubim wings
made for showing off
with a violin or baton

My mother inherited the hands of my grandfather Arturo,
small and knotty, with blunt fingers.

De tantas manos que se han venido juntando
saqué estas manos.
¿De quién tengo las uñas, los dedos,
los nudillos, las palmas, las frágiles muñecas?

Cuando acaricio tu espalda,
las óseas salientes de tus pies
tus largas piernas sólidas,
¿Qué manos a través de mis manos te acarician?

From so many hands coming together
I ended up with these.
From whom did I get the fingers, nails,
knuckles and palms, the fragile wrists?

When I caress your back,
the bony protrusions of your feet,
your long sturdy legs,
what hands through my hands caress you?

AGUACERO

Desde una ventana hermética de oficina
contemplo el aguacero.
Sobre el cinc herrumbroso
ruedan flores amarillas
de alguna acacia que se sacude al viento.

Como pez en pecera
diviso con envidia a la chavala que fui
empapada y feliz, saltando
lodazales y desoyendo llamados
para que después
      la alcahueta tía-abuela
a escondidas del abuelo
me secara la cabellera,
me cambiara la ropa,
me limpiara de lodo los zapatos.
Y arrebujada en colchas
tibias como el cariño,
         me dormía

¡Un viejo aguacero que logra mojarme
         sólo por dentro,

DOWNPOUR

From an airtight office window
I gaze out at the downpour.
Yellow flowers
from an acacia shaken by the wind
roll along a rusty tin roof.

A fish in a fishbowl
I recall with envy the young girl who was
drenched and happy, jumping
mud puddles and ignoring calls
because later
       my go-between great aunt
hidden from grandfather
would dry my hair,
change my clothes,
clean the mud off my shoes.
And wrapped up in a bedspread
warm as love
       I slept.

An old downpour that succeeds in soaking me
       only within

está golpeando el cinc,
y ya colma canales y bajantes
y el lecho de la memoria!

is now beating the tin roof,
flooding the canals and levies
and the riverbed of memory!

ESPEJO DE MANO

Después de tantos años,
mi abuela Ilse regresa
con sus asombrados ojos
oscuros y tristones y se asoma
    — grácil Narciso —
su pequeño estanque de plata,
a su óvalo mágico,
a su luna de cristal cortado,
ocupando este rostro
cada vez más suyo
             y menos mío.

HAND MIRROR

After so many years
my grandmother Ilse returns
with her astonished
dark and melancholy eyes,
and glances
    — slender Narcissus —
at her small silver pool,
her magic oval,
her moon of cut glass,
occupying this face
more and more hers
                and less mine.

FAMILIA

> "Vuestra felicidad está hecha de halago
> y de silencio, dulzura y cobardía."
> Ernesto Mejía Sánchez

Después no vayan a decir que no los busqué
que no quise acercarme
que nunca se sabe conmigo a qué atenerse,
cuando al atravesar lo más ardiente del desierto
         ustedes mismos
        me negaron agua.

FAMILY

> "Your happiness is made of flattery
> and silence, sweetness and cowardice."
> Ernesto Mejía Sanchez

Don't say later that I didn't look for you
that I didn't want to get close
that no one ever knows what to expect from me,
when on crossing the hottest part of the desert
        you yourselves
        denied me water.

LOS ZAPATOS VIEJOS

En un rincón te esperan
conocedores de todas las vueltas de tu vida,
aunque ya quisieras acabarlos;
preferís otros zapatos
que ahora te parecen mejor.

Pero el tiempo los ha hecho
molde de tus pies:
curva de tu talón izquierdo.
Nada ni nadie como ellos se ajustan
tanto a vos y a tu manera.

Más fieles que todas tus mujeres,
más fieles que todos tus amigos,
más fieles que algunos de tu parentela.

OLD SHOES

In a corner they await you,
connoisseurs of all your life's wanderings,
even though you'd like to get rid of them:
you prefer other shoes
that now look better to you.

But time has made them
a mold of your feet:
the contour of your left heel.
Nothing and no one conforms
to you and your ways more than they.

More faithful than all your women,
more faithful than all your friends,
more faithful than some of your relatives.

(MP/BP)

SALUD, VIEJO

Supongo que tu infierno habrá sido peor
que el que me hiciste padecer.
Así me dejaste
a que me defienda como pueda,
ya nunca podré ser la que debiera haber sido.
Pero ahora estás muerto
y ya tengo edad para perdonarte.

La verdad es que dispusiste de tu vida
como te dio la gana.
Tendrías sesenta años bien cumplidos,
pero preferiste bebértelos de un sorbo.
                              ¡Salud, viejo!

CHEERS, OLD MAN

I suppose your hell was worse
than the one you inflicted on me.
You left me
to defend myself as I could,
and I'll never be what I should have been.
But now you're dead
and I'm old enough to forgive you.

The truth is that you lived your life
just as you pleased.
You could have had sixty full years
but you preferred to drink them in one gulp.
                    Cheers, old man!

REFLEXIÓN SOBRE MIS PIES

Tengo los pies de mi padre:
delgados, largos, pálidos pies de venas azulosas;
                              huesudos pies de hombre
distintos de los pies de mis hermanas
                    redondos, suaves,
                              leves pies de mujer.

Mis pies estrechos como espátulas
que usaron calcetines y zapatos escueleros
traficaron corredores, algarabías de clases y recreos;
estrenaron medias, sandalias finas, charol, gamuza
y los primeros tacones de los bailes.

Alguna huella habrá quedado de estos pies
en el sitio del combate.
                    Algún rastro
en las empinadas calles sube-y-baja de Tegucigalpa,
oscuras en la noche o desiertas de madrugada;
en las siempre húmedas avenidas de San José
                    al cambio de luz en los semáforos;
en el caramanchel de la clandestina Radio Sandino,
en los buses, las ventas, las comiderías, los mercados,

REFLECTING ON MY FEET

I have my father's feet:
thin, long, pale feet with blue veins;
         the bony feet of a man
distinct from my sisters' feet,
        the round, smooth,
            soft feet of a woman

My feet, narrow as spatulas,
wore schoolgirl's shoes and socks
maneuvered corridors, the uproar of classes and recess;
wore stockings for the first time, delicate sandals, patent
                        leather,
and my first high heels for dances.

These feet will have left a footprint
in the combat zone,
        a trace
in the steep up-and-down streets of Tegucigalpa,
dark at night or deserted at dawn;
in the ever humid streets of San Jose
        at the changing of a traffic light;
in the shack housing clandestine Radio Sandino,
in the buses, inns, restaurants, and markets,

las casas de seguridad.
        en el hospital clandestino.

Se reivindicaron mis pies con mocasines,
zapatos tennis y botas
           chapaleando charcos
con el bluyín, la camisa y el pelo eternamente húmedos
— el exilio es un recuerdo mohoso y catarriento —

Miro estos pies que ahora caminan libremente
on sandalias, tacones o botas de miliciana.
El hueso del empeine lo tengo de mi abuelo
y ya no sé desde cuándo vendré caminando
sembradas las plantas de mis pies
           en esta tierra nuestra,
esta tierra de todos, entregada a todos
para construir con ella
           el futuro de todos.

the safe houses,
                in the clandestine hospital.

My feet have recuperated with moccasins,
tennis shoes and boots
                splashing in puddles
with shirt and hair perpetually damp
— exile is a choked and moldy memory —

I see these feet that now walk freely
in sandals, high heels, or military boots.
I have my grandfather's instep
and I don't know how long I've been walking,
the soles of my feet planted
                in this earth of ours,
this earth, given to everyone
to build the future.

QUERIDA TÍA CHOFI

a Adilia Moncada

No eras la tía Chofi del poema de Jaime Sabines,
pero también te llamabas Sofía, Chofi.
Vos, la rebelde desde chiquita,
la que se casó contra todo el mundo
pero con su hombre. Aunque la vida
después resultara un purgatorio e infierno
hasta que Guillermo terminó desnucándose borracho
para tu descanso. Y concluiste
otro capítulo de tu vida
que yo te escuchaba contar, fascinada
mientras hacías escarchas de azúcar de colores
que secabas al sol en láminas de vidrio.

Artesana, Imaginera, Panadera, Decoradora,
poblaste tu mundo de enanos, Blancanieves,
Cenicientas, Niñas de 15 años,
Parejas de Primera Comunión, Casamientos
Tiernos de Bautizo,
entre tules, perlas, filigranas,
ramilletes, cintas y lazos de pastillaje.

BELOVED AUNT CHOFI

for Adilia Moncada

You weren't the Aunti Chofi of Jaime Sabines' poem
but your name was also Sofia, Chofi.
You, rebellious since childhood, who against everyone's
            wishes
married her man. Even though life
later turned into purgatory and hell
until William ended up drunkenly breaking his neck
and gave you some rest. And you wrapped up
another chapter in your life,
which I listened to you recount, fascinated,
while you made colored sugar candy
that you dried in the sun on sheets of glass.

Craftswoman, Image Maker, Baker, Decorator,
you peopled your world with dwarves, Snow White,
Cinderella, 15-year-old Girls,
First Communion Couples, Marriages,
Baptized Infants,
in the midst of tulle, pearls, filligree,
bouquets, ribbons, and swirls of frosting.

Los sacuanjoches sacados de panas de agua
se convertían en tus manos en coronas,
diademas y cetros frescos
— efímeros símbolos de efímeros reinados.
Los mediodías eran la penumbra de tu cuarto
contra el solazo. Tu aposento lleno de pinceles,
óleos moldes de yeso,
caballetes, lienzos, bastidores,
santos de bulto a medio retocar,
y en medio del caos, tu cama eternamente desarreglada.
Habladora, Conversadora, platicabas mientras ibas
fumando cigarrillos,
encendiendo uno con la colilla del otro
hasta dejar tu cuarto como un cenicero lleno
de colillas retorcidas y fragante a tazas de café,
miel, azúcar, harina, claras de huevo,
trementina, aceite de linaza,
sábanas viejas.

Amazona admirable en tus fantásticas hazañas:
(amarraste al ebrio de tu marido,

The *sacuanjoches*† scooped out of water bowls
in your hands became crowns,
diadems, and fresh scepters for beauty queens
— ephemeral symbols of ephemeral kingdoms.
Midday was the penumbra in your bedroom
against the scorching sun. Your room filled with
paintbrushes,
oils, plaster molds,
easels, canvases, frames,
half-finished figures of saints,
and in the middle of the chaos, your
perpetually unmade bed.
Great Talker. Conversationalist. You chatted while you
smoked cigarettes,
lighting one with the tail end of another
until your room ended up like an ashtray full
of crushed cigarette butts, smelling of coffee,
honey, sugar, flour, egg whites,
turpentine, linseed oil,
old sheets.

Amazon, admirable for your fantastic feats:
(you tied up your husband in his drunkenness,

†national flower of Nicaragua

31

te amaste con el primer Gurú legítimo de la India
que pasó por Managua).
Curandera, hacías medicinas, jarabes y pócimas terribles
que nos obligabas a beber
contra todas las enfermedades posibles.

Recorrías Managua bajo aquel solazo
con tu cartera repleta de chunches,
el pelo alborotado
y la eterna brasa entre los labios.

Qué necesidad, qué desgracia no ayudaste:
Partera, Enfermera,
alistabas muertos, atendías borrachos,
defendías causas perdidas desde siempre
y en todas las discusiones familiares
gobernaba tu figura desgarbada.

Siempre en tránsito, viviste
en cuartos alquilados,
te salvaste de milagro en los terremotos
y cualquier persona soportó cualquier barbaridad tuya.
Te peleaste hasta con la guardia
y fuiste a parar al exilio de México.

you fell under the spell of the first
legitimate Indian guru
who passed through Managua).
Healer, you brewed medicine, potions, and terrible
                                    concoctions
that you made us drink
to guard against all possible ailments.

You ran around Managua under the scorching sun
with your purse full of watchmacallits,
your hair wild and free
and that perpetual ember between your lips.

No need or misfortune did you fail to aid:
Midwife, Nurse,
you prepared the dead, took care of drunks,
defended lost causes all your life
and your ungraceful figure
led every family discussion.

Always in transit, you lived in rented rooms,
miraculously survived earthquakes
and everyone had to endure your rudeness.
You even argued with the National Guard
and fled in exile to Mexico.

A veces, con tus manos pequeñitas y regordetas
de puntas afiladas, como manos de bebé
o como palmeritas de abanico en miniatura,
te arreglabas el pelo entrecano
con una onda sobre la frente
y en ese gesto rápido, fugazmente
se vislumbraba tu antigua gracia.

Porque un día de verdad que fuiste hermosa,
morena y altiva.
Nada tenía que ver esa joven con vos misma:
Oveja Negra, Paja en ojos ajenos,
Vergüenza de tu única hija
— que a pulso enviaste a estudiar a México —
y de allí saltó a Pittsburg, a New York,
y recorrió Europa acumulando becas
y títulos académicos
con nostalgias de supuestos linajes
para borrarte, para no verte,
para no tener que sufrirte.
¡Ah! pero vos te llenabas la boca con su nombre.

La mañana antes de tu muerte
estuviste igual que siempre, gritona y bocatera
sólo que te quejaste
de mucho malestar en los riñones.

Sometimes, your tiny plump hands with pointed finger tips,
like the hands of a boy
or like little palm trees fanned out in miniature,
arranged your graying hair
in a wave over your forehead
and this quick gesture, gave
a fleeting glimpse of your former charms.

Because one day, truly, you were beautiful,
dark and haughty
That young girl had nothing to do with you yourself.
Black sheep, speck in the eye,
Shame of your only daughter
— for whom you slaved so you could send her to study in
                                        Mexico —
from there she leapt to Pittsburg, New York,
traveled all over Europe accumulating scholarships
and academic degrees
yearning for so-called nobility
to blur you, avoid you
not have to put up with you.
Ah! But your mouth was filled with her name.

The morning before your death
you were the same as ever, loud-mouthed and hollering,
but you complained of discomfort in your kidneys

(Tu hija supo la noticia en Buenos Aires).

Vos que me contabas de tus trances en el espejo,
tus reencarnaciones
— múltiples vidas de las que recordabas
incontables anécdotas:
(En una de tus vidas fuiste una niña que murió
recién nacida, en otra, un hombre aventurero . . .)

¿En qué vida estás ahora
que ya no te llamás Sofía,
          Sabia, Sabiduría,
ahora que te llamás huesos, madera desvencijada,
podredumbre, tierra vegetal,
humus, fosa, oscuridad.
                    nada?

Ahora que ya no estás, que ya no existís
quizás te reconozcás

                    en este espejo.

(Your daughter heard the news in Buenos Aires.)

You told me about your trances in the mirror
your reincarnations
— multiple lives from which you remembered
innumerable anecdotes:
(In one of your lives you were a newborn child who died,
in another an adventurer . . .)

What life are you in now
now that your name isn't Sofia
            Sabia, Sabiduría
now that your name is bones, rotten wood,
putrefaction, vegetal earth,
humus, grave, darkness,
                              nothing?

Now that you are not, now that you don't exist
perhaps you recognize yourself
                              in this mirror.

PREÑEZ

Esta inesperada redondez,
este perder mi cintura de ánfora
y hacerme tinaja,
es regresar al barro, al sol, al aguacero
y entender cómo germina la semilla
en la humedad caliente de mi tierra.

PREGNANCY

This unexpected roundness
this losing my hourglass figure
and turning into a jug,
is to return to clay, sun, rain
and to understand how seed germinates
in my hot, humid earth.

(MP/BP)

AL PARTO

> "¡Ah, dice, cómo en el cristal diviso
> a lo que más eterno resplandece,
> puede ser escarmiento de ceniza!"
> Luis de Sandoval Zapata

Desperté con aquellos espasmos.
Desde mi vientre llamaban hacia afuera.
Sólo el dolor iba expandiéndose y replegándose
como un oleaje cada vez más agitado.

Me levanté ya con torpeza
abarcando con mis brazos el océano;
sosteniendo, abrazando aquel inmenso corazón
convulso y expectante
                    hasta alcanzar la ducha matinal
porque ya rompían las aguas: la fuente.
Se dejaba venir el torrente incontenible de la vida.

Pero ya frente al espejo
al peinarme el pelo
empapado, chorréandome sobre las clavículas,
vi mis ojos inmersos en pura transparencia
su verde translúcido de iris resplandeciente

CHILDBIRTH

> "Ah, what I in the mirror behold
> as glowing most eternally
> may be a warning of ash."
> Luis de Sandoval Zapata

I awoke with spasms
calling out from my womb,
delivering only pain, doubling over and building
like a rush of waves, more and more agitated.

Sluggish, I arose,
embracing the ocean;
Sustaining, clasping that immense
convulsive, expectant heart
            even getting my morning shower
because my waters had already broken: the fountain.
The uncontrollable torrent of life was let loose.

But facing the mirror,
combing my drenched
hair dripping on my collar bones,
I saw my eyes immersed in pure clarity
the translucent green of their radiant iris

sobre las ojeras, los altos pómulos, la frente comba,
como si tras la piel, mi propio cráneo
me enfrentara con el rostro de la muerte.

over dark circles, high cheekbones, curved brow,
as if beneath the skin, my own skull
were confronting me with death's face.

(MP/BP)

HIJA

Como hojita de sauce
                    o de bambú
te me pegás
buscando mi sombra
                    frágil.

DAUGHTER

Like a little leaf of willow
                    or bamboo
you stick to me
looking for my delicate
                    shadow.

MARÍA DENISE

Apretada contra mi pecho
dondequiera que voy
              te llevo.

No hemos tenido sitio fijo de reposo:
Los tibios atardeceres del verano,
los aguaceros de Junio,
las madrugadas lluviosas de Octubre
los vientos de Diciembre,
en cualquier parte nos encuentran
siempre acomodadas la una a la otra.

Mi mejor premio es tu sonrisa
Pajarito Chino,
              Angel Verde
sin más alas que te acurruquen
              que mis brazos.

MARÍA DENISE

Pressed against my breast
I take you
              wherever I go.

We haven't had the chance to settle down:
Summer's cool evenings,
June showers,
rainy October dawns
December winds,
wherever they find us
we're always at home with each other.

My best prize is your smile
Little Chinese Bird
              Green Angel
with no other wings to nestle you
              than my arms.

(MP/BP)

ARRURÚ PARA UNA MUERTA RECIÉN NACIDA

¿Cómo hubiera sido tu sonrisa?
¿Qué habrías aprendido a decir primero?
¡Tanta esperanza para nada!
Tuve que secar mis pechos que te esperaban.

Una fotografía apresurada
insinúa tu limpio perfil,
la breve boca.
Pero no puedo recordar cómo eras,
cómo habrías sido.

Tan viva te sentí, dándote vueltas
protegida en mi vientre.
Ahora me despierto estremecida
en medio de la noche
— hueco el vientre —
y me aferro a un impreciso primer llanto
que escuché anestesiada
en el quirófano.

LULLABY FOR A DEAD NEWBORN

What would your smile have looked like?
What would your first word have been?
So much hoping for nothing!
My expectant breasts had to dry up.

A hasty photo
suggests your clear profile,
your tiny mouth.
But I can't recall how you were,
how you would have been.

I felt you so alive, moving around,
safe in my belly.
Now I wake up shivering
in the middle of the night
— my womb hollow —
and cling to that indistinct
first cry I heard, anesthetized,
in the operating room.

CAMPO ARRASADO

La maleta de su ropita que guardé con tanto
cuidado,
la niña que cruza la calle en brazos de su
madre,
o la visión efímera de una mujer preñada
esperando bus.

Cualquier encuentro / Chispa / Desata la
hoguera
de este desprevenido corazón: zacate seco,
yesca
que se reduce a cenizas humeantes, a
campo arrasado.

RAZED EARTH

The suitcase full of baby clothes I kept with such
                              care,
a little girl crossing the street in her
                              mother's arms,
or a passing glance at a pregnant woman
                              waiting for a bus.

Any encounter / Spark / Unleashes
                              a bonfire
in this unprepared heart: dry fodder,
                              tinder
reduced to smokey ash, to
                              razed earth.

(MP/BP)

VOCES AMADAS

Aquella tarde que llamaste a María Mercedes
descubrí en tu voz la voz de tu padre
a quien nunca conocí.

Hubo un instante
que hablaste con una voz que no era tuya.

Una voz
       eco de otra voz
que tu hermana mayor, Gladys
       recordaría
o tu madre (si viviera)
habría reconocido de inmediato.

BELOVED VOICES

That afternoon when you called María Mercedes
I discovered in your voice the voice of your father
whom I never knew.

There was a moment
when you spoke with a voice that wasn't yours.

A voice
      echo of another voice
that your older sister, Gladys,
      would remember
or your mother (if she were living)
would have recognized immediately.

EL GATO

No se sabe cómo apareció.
En las mañanas se estira al sol
o miramos ondular su silueta
tras el vidrio opaco de la ventana.

Ingrimo, como nosotros:
"una pareja expuesta al dardo . . ."

Es tierra de nadie, macho sin dueña,
gato de contil
      que sobrevive
      cazando cucarachas
         y algún ratón.

CAT

No one knows where he came from.
In the morning he stretches in the sun,
or we watch his silhouette undulate
behind the opaque glass in the window.

Lonely like us:
"a couple struck by the arrow . . ."

He's no one's property, does as he pleases,
this charcoal cat
          who survives
          catching cockroaches
                    and an occasional rat.

OTRO TIEMPO

Regresamos al lugar donde fuimos felices
acompañados de nuevos amigos;
sentados uno frente al otro
tu mano ya no busca mi mano bajo la mesa.

A la sombra
están vacías las mesas que antes ocupábamos.
El mediodía blanquea los icacos en las más altas ramas
las guayabas verdean entre las hojas verdes.

Hay cordialidad entre nosotros
parecemos dos viejos amigos.
Con ternura, preñada de tristeza
miro las mesas y las sillas, muertas y solas.

ANOTHER TIME

We return to the place we were happy
accompanied by new friends:
seated face to face
your hand no longer seeks mine under the table.

In the shade
the tables where we once sat are empty.
Midday whitens the cocoplums in the highest branches
guayabas grow green among green leaves.

There's warmth between us,
we look like two old friends.
Tenderly, pregnant with sadness,
I look at the tables and chairs, so dead and alone.

(MP/BP)

LA MESERA (1)

De mesa en mesa
recoge las botellas vacías de cerveza,
apila los platos en la bandeja plástica
y sus gruesos dedos como pinzas
levantan de una vez
cinco vasos de vidrio
que hacen "clic" al juntarse.

Como un cometa gordo recorre su órbita:
el trajín enciende su rostro
agita sus brazos y los pequeños pechos
bajo el vestido celeste con delantal
que le termina en lazo
             sobre las ancas.

Va
             de mesa
                          en mesa
hasta que las pláticas se arralan,
se apagan los ruidos de la cocina
y los clientes se dispersan.
Dejan de pasar los buses

THE WAITRESS (1)

From table to table
she gathers empty beer bottles,
piles plates on a plastic tray.
Her thick fingers like tongs
pick up five glasses at once
that "click" when they come together.

Like a fat comet she makes the rounds:
the coming and going flushes her face,
stirs up her arms and her tiny breasts
under the sky-blue dress with an apron
tied over her hips.

She goes
              from table
                            to table
until the chatting dies down,
the kitchen noises cease
and the customers go home.
The buses stop running

y la luna se ve alta
sobre los postes de luz.

Al cerrar,
ella coloca las sillas sobre las mesas
y se sienta al fondo de la comidería.
Con dificultad se saca los zapatos,
encarama los pies sobre el taburete
y voltea las bolsas de su delantal
       para contar

              una por una
              las monedas del día.

and the moon hangs high
above the lampposts.

Closing up
she stacks the chairs on the tables
and sits down at the end of the counter.
Sighing, she takes off her shoes,
puts her feet up on the stool
and empties her apron pockets
       to count
               the day's tips.
               one by one

LA COSTURERA

Toda mi vida sobre una Singer 15-30
y en las noches soñando pespuntes,
jaretas, hilvanes
mangas, vuelos, paletones.
Ni tiempo tuve para hombres
siempre cansada y con dolor en la columna.

Yo que era una chavala tan alegre,
la hija mayor, la preferida de mi padre.
Después que me arruinó tu papa
ya no tuve juventud
sólo trabajo y más trabajo.

Te di vida, hijo,
pero yo no he tenido vida,
y ya ni sé cómo hubiera sido
de haber sido yo misma.

SEAMSTRESS

All my life bent over a Singer 15-30,
all night dreaming of backstitches,
hems, basting,
sleeves, ruffles, zippers.
I never had time for men:
always tired, with an aching back.

I was once a happy young girl,
the oldest daughter, my father's pet.
After your father disgraced me,
I no longer had my youth,
just work and more work.

I gave you life, my son,
but I've not had life,
and I have no idea how it would have been
to have been myself.

LA MESERA (2)

Cómo creía entonces que de verdad
para algo me serviría el físico.
Morena y delgadita
sólo por mí venían los montones de clientes
desde Managua y Los Pueblos,
ya no se diga los que entraban
de aquí de Masaya.
Me tocaban las nalgas y tenía
ofertas al escoger:
De amorcito para arriba me trataban.

Claro que me acuerdo de vos, Castillito;
desde que te fuiste a México a estudiar
siempre pedí a los amigos
razón tuya.

Ya ves, cómo me tienen los muchachos:
gorda, cansada y varicosa.
Ni estoy tan vieja
pero así son las cosas de la vida;

La mesera más linda del "Mini-16 Rojo"
y de qué me sirvió.

THE WAITRESS (2)

Once I truly believed that
my looks would be good for something.
Only for me, because I was dark and slender,
did the hordes of customers
come from Managua and Los Pueblos
not to mention those from here in Masaya.
They patted my ass
and I got lots of offers:
It started with sweet talk and went on from there

Of course, I remember you, Castillito,
after you left to study in Mexico
I always asked your friends
about you.

Now you see how the boys have left me:
tired and fat, with varicose veins.
I'm not even very old
but that's life.

The prettiest waitress in the Red Mini-16
And what good did it do me?

OTILIA PLANCHADORA

Al ritmo de la Sonora Matancera
Otilia pringa la ropa,
la dobla en grandes tinas de aluminio
                    y panas enlozadas,
la estira sobre la mesa
y no sé si baila o plancha
                    al son cadencioso.

"Los aretes que le faltan a la luna . . ."
Otilia los llevó puestos al baile
                    del Club de Obreros.

(Ella tenía novio de bigotito)

Otilia, frutal y esquiva,
entallada por el vestido
bailó, bailó, hasta que se humedecieron
oscuros sus sobacos entalcados.

En la barraca del fondo
— bodega de tabaco, cuarto de planchar,
    albergue del relente de las noches
que refresca las tardes de verano,

OTILIA IRONING

To the rhythm of Sonora Matancera
Otilia sprinkles the clothes,
folds them in large aluminum tubs
                    and enameled vats,
spreads them out on the table,
and I don't know whether she's dancing or ironing
                    to the rhythmic sound.

"The earrings missing from the moon . . . "
Otilia wore them to the dance
                    at the Workers Club.

(She had a boyfriend with a little mustache.)

Otilia, earthy and shy,
hugged by her dress,
danced and danced, until her powdered arm pits
moistened and darkened.

In the shed in back
— tobacco shop, ironing room,
    shelter from the chill night breeze
that refreshes summer evenings,

Otilia guarda su plancha.
Sueña que Bienvenido Granda
                    y Celio González
cantan para ella "Novia mía"
mientras se pringa la cara con lágrimas.

Otilia puts her iron away,
and dreams that Bienvenido Granda
                    and Celio González
sing "Novia Mia" for her
while she sprinkles her face with tears.

LA MESERA (3)

Con delantal y uniforme
como las otras
pasa todo el día atendiendo órdenes:
"Dos cervezas, un coctel de camarones;
la malteada de chocolate
    un banana split,
            un arcoiris."

De un extremo a otro de la barra
sirve agua, pica hielo,
prepara dos vasos de té al mismo tiempo.
Abre el congelador, saca el helado
mezcla leche, destapa cervezas;
arregla el coctel, tira las tapas al suelo,
coloca todo sobre la barra y sirve.

Parece igual a las otras
pero es distinta:
            resplandece
cuando el novio atisba
tras la puerta de vidrio
    de la cafetería.

THE WAITRESS (3)

In an apron and uniform
like the others
she spends all day filling orders:
"two beers, a shrimp cocktail;
a chocolate malt
    a banana split,
        a float."

From one end of the counter to the other
she pours water, cracks ice,
prepares two glasses of tea at the same time.
She opens the freezer, takes out ice cream,
stirs milk, opens beers;
she fixes cocktails, throws bottle caps on the floor,
puts everything on the counter and serves.

She looks like the others
but she's different:
                she glows
when her boyfriend peeks
from behind the glass door
        of the cafeteria.

MUCHACHA CON SOMBRILLA

De overol amarillo
cruza la calle
— las grandes nalgas al ritmo
                    de su paso —

La sudorosa espalda
                    bajo su blusa roja
y el gran girasol
                    de su sombrilla.

GIRL WITH UMBRELLA

Wearing yellow overalls
she crosses the street
— her big buttocks in rhythm
                    with her step —

Her sweaty back
                    beneath her red blouse
and the big sunflower
                    of her umbrella.

FIEL AMA DE CASA

Todo terminó con la Luna de Miel:
Azahares, cartas de amor, llantos pueriles.

Ahora reptas a los pies de tu señor:
Primera en su harén,
tomada o abandonada según capricho.
Madre de los hijos de su apellido
oreando tu abandono
          junto al tendedero de pañales,
estrujando tu corazón
          hasta despercudirlo en la ropa blanca.
Acostumbrada al grito, a la humiliación
de la mano servil ante la dádiva,
Mujer arrinconada
          Sombra quejumbrosa
con jaquecas, várices, diabetes.

Niña guardada en estuche
que casó con primer novio
y envejeció escuchando el lejano bullicio
de la vida desde su sitial de esposa.

FAITHFUL HOUSEWIFE

Everything ended with the Honeymoon:
orange blossoms, love letters, childish tears.

Now you crawl at the feet of your lord:
Number one in his harem,
taken or abandoned at his whim.
Mother of children with his last name
airing your neglect
          near the clothesline of diapers,
wringing your heart
          until it washes out with the white clothing.
Accustomed to the loud voice, the humiliation
of a subservient hand before the gift,
Cornered woman
          Wailing shadow
with migraines, varicose veins, and diabetes.

A little girl kept in a jewelry box
married her first boyfriend
and grew old listening to the distant din of life
from her honorable place of wife.

LETANÍAS POR LA CHANITA

Animalito doméstico, Palomita en jaula,
Niña sin memoria de la madre:
— "De mi mamá no me acuerdo del todito . . ." —
Desde los seis años sirviendo en la casa patriarcal.
Banquito, Comodín, Mecedora,
Almohadilla para aliviar el cansancio de los pies de todos;
Avara de postres y golosinas
que los niños de la casa, saciados en su gula
apartaban con desgano.
Nunca una mano entrañable, un brazo, un ala tibia
acurrucó tu cabeza, levantó tu barbilla,
pellizcó tus cachetes
de niña mofletuda y colochona.
Sin partida ni lugar de nacimiento:
— "Creo que nací en Jinotepe . . ." —
        Sin edad,
— "No sé cuántos años tengo . . ." —
Descalza, analfabeta.
Adolescente que habrá guardado íngrima
terrores y equívocos ante el ardor de la carne.
De misas a la aurora y rezos vespertinos,
envuelta en rebozos y faldas anchas
sobre toscos fustanes.

LITANIES FOR LA CHANITA

Little pet, caged Dove,
Girl with no memory of a mother:
— "I don't remember a thing about my mother . . ." —
Serving in a patriarchal home since the age of six.
Footstool, Comforter, Rocking Chair.
Cushion for alleviating the weariness of everyone's feet;
Greedy for desserts and sweets
that the children of the house, satiated in their gluttony,
pushed away with indifference.
Never did a beloved hand, an arm, a warm wing
cradle your head, lift your chin,
pinch the chubby cheeks
of the curly-haired girl.
Without birthplace or certificate:
— "I think I was born in Jinotepe . . ." —
        Without age,
— "I don't know how old I am . . ." —
Barefoot, illiterate.
Adolescent who must have harbored lonely
terrors and misconceptions about the ardor of the flesh.
From early morning masses to evening prayers
wrapped in shawls and ample skirts
over cheap, coarse petticoats.

Tu camastro recogió soledades, llantos,
bajo la luz mortecina de la lámpara
de aquel último cuarto / palomar / alto de tablas.
Te consolaste amando hijos ajenos
                    rubios, hermosos y exigentes.

Pelo acomodado en una redecilla cien veces zurcida,
Manos ásperas y sin uñas
                    blancuzcas de almidón
                    de tanto lavar y lavar.
Tu música era el molenillo batiendo los deliciosos
                    refrescos de la mañana.
Tu mayor orgullo: los corredores
que relumbraban como vitrales
                    con el sol de la tarde.

Cuerpo de raíz, encorvado y rugoso,
sobreviviste todas las desgracias.
Y cuando te hablo de la Revolución y del futuro,
permanecés callada y sonriente
con los últimos dientes que te quedan.

Your poor wretched bed collected loneliness and sobs
in the dying light from the lamp
in that furthermost room / pigeon coop / platform of boards.
You consoled yourself by loving another's children
                    blond, beautiful and demanding.

Hair gathered in a net darned a hundred times.
Hands rough, without fingernails
                    whitened by starch
                    from endless washing.
Your music was the whisk beating delicious
                    morning drinks.
Your greatest pride: the hallways
that shone like stained-glass windows
                        in afternoon sun.

Body of root, stooped and wrinkled,
you survived all the misfortunes.
And when I talk to you about the Revolution and the future,
you remain silent, smiling
through your last remaining teeth.

(MP/BP)

AFEITES DE LA MUERTE

a Nora Astorga

Ahora querés apartar la muerte con un ademán
como espantando una mosca real o imaginaria.
Ya te sabés el desahucio: el diagnóstico, la biopsia positiva
las señales inequívocas.
Pero seguís haciéndote como que no las ves,
ignorando lo sabido deliberadamente,
hablando de asuntos superfluos / frivolidades.

Esa mascarilla, su falsa tersura:
rosa escarchado en tus mejillas,
perfumado borgoña humedeciendo tus labios,
relámpagos de azul y oro sobre los párpados
son los límites del milagro / Pero tras los cosméticos
está Ella,
remontando a través del lienzo
las capas de pintura que se cuartean y desprenden.

Profundizás el juego y todos te seguimos cortesmtente /
complicidad crispada /
con la vista oscurecida por el siniestro resplandor.

DEATHLY MAKEUP

For Nora Astorga

You want to push aside death with a gesture
as if shooing away a real or imaginary fly.
You learn of the eviction: the diagnosis, the positive biopsy,
the unmistakable signs.
But you act as if you see nothing,
deliberately ignoring the known,
talking about superfluous matters / frivolities.

That death mask, its fake gloss:
frosty pink on your cheeks,
fragrant burgundy moistening your lips,
blue and gold flashes on your eyelids
are the limits of the miracle / But behind the cosmetics
there She is,
overcoming the canvas,
the coats of paint that crack and loosen.

You go deep into the game and politely we follow /
tensely complicit /
vision dimmed by the ominous blaze.

Cómo quisiera verte en otros tiempos
como en aquella foto que recorrió el mundo:
(Encarnación del futuro, Esperanza viva
                                    en verde-olivo).

Contabilizo la memoria
como el avaro atesora miserables monedas:
La infancia que compartimos de abuelas hacendosas
y ceremoniosos abuelos de lino y jipijapa
que nos soportaban con benevolencia y ternura.
La adolescencia plagada de equívocos y fantasías;
la edad de las conspiraciones, de los contactos,
        de ser la carnada del operativo,
el desarraigo y el exilio como precio de la acción;
después, hombres amados / hijos / desgracias mutuas.

¿Qué no cambiarías ahora por la vida?
Pero ya no me atrevo a preguntarte nada
como si no tuvieras angustias ni pesares.
Desafiante, como un James Dean
en tu traje tachonado de estrellas
lleno de zípperes metálicos
tu cuerpo rebelde, ya en su funda /
        negándose a la muerte.

How I'd like to see you as in other times,
as in that photo that went round the world:
(Soul of the future, living Hope

                                in olive-green).

I count up my memories
the way a miser hoards miserable money:
A childhood we shared with hardworking grandmothers
and formal grandfathers in linen suits and panama hats,
who endured us with kindness and tenderness.
An adolescence full of ambiguity and fantasy,
the age of conspiracies, contacts, being the bait of the
        operative,
uprooting and exile as the price of action;
and later, lovers / children / mutual misfortunes.

What wouldn't you give now for life?
But I dare not ask you,
as if you had no worries or regrets.
Defiant, like James Dean
in your star-studded dress
full of metallic zippers
your rebel body, now in its case /
                denying death.

BLANCA ARÁUZ

La conocí al comenzar la guerra,
intimé con ella
y tomando café y platicando por la tarde
y a veces toda la noche
                    hasta el alba
nos dimos cuenta que pensábamos igual.

Un sólo cuerpo. Un mismo pensamiento.
                    Éramos como dos lámparas
— además de la lámpara Coleman
que alumbraba las tablas encaladas del telégrafo —
aunque no estuviéramos juntos,
aunque pasáramos cinco años separados,
ella en San Rafael, yo en estas montañas.

Dos luces buscándose, haciéndose señas
                    llamándose
a través de pantanos, a través de la noche
      y los árboles
para iluminarse uno con el otro.

BLANCA ARÁUZ

I met her at the beginning of the war,
we became close;
drinking coffee and talking all afternoon
and sometimes all night
                    until dawn
we realized we thought alike.

A single body. The same ideas.
                    We were like two lamps
— besides the Coleman lantern
that lit up the whitewashed planks of the telegraph office —
even though we weren't together,
even though we spent five years apart,
she in San Rafael, I in these mountains

Two lights seeking each other, sending signals,
                    calling out
across the marshes, through night and trees
        to illuminate one another.

VOY A HABLAR DE MIS MUJERES

Toda esta tierra sabe sus nombres de memoria:
El Chipote, La Chispa, la gruta de Tunagualán
recuerdan sus nombres y a veces los confían al viento . . .

        Cómo no recordar a Emilia
la enfermera, con una puntería como su mano
para las jeringas, que dio cuenta de tres gringos.
Se tronó al primero a un kilómetro de distancia
y por la manera de caer — según Pancho Estrada —
le dio en la cabeza.
El segundo cayó seis semanas después.
Yo no lo vi, pero lo atestiguó el General Irías
y dos semanas más tarde se tronó al tercero.
Después se ha dedicado a curar, a inyectar, a vacunar . . .
Hasta Honduras se cruza en mula
a traer sus medicamentos
y no tiene miedo de atravesar íngrima esas montañas.
¡Ah, la Emilia! Tan distinta pero igual a otras mujeres . . .

LET ME TALK ABOUT MY WOMEN

This whole land knows their names by heart:
El Chipote, La Chispa, the cave at Tunagualán
remember their names and sometimes entrust them to the
                              wind . . .

                    Who could forget Emilia
the nurse, whose aim, like her hand with
a syringe, accounted for three dead gringos.
She shot the first at a kilometer's distance
and judging by the way he fell—according to Pancho
          Estrada—
she got him in the head.
The second fell six weeks later.
I didn't see it, but General Irías affirmed it,
and two weeks later she shot the third.
Since then she's been dedicated to healing, to giving shots
                    and vaccinations . . .
Traveling as far as Honduras by mule
to bring back medicine,
she's not afraid to cross those mountains alone.
Ah, Emilia! So different from other women, yet the same.

Cómo no mencionar
a la Juana Cruz, cantinera jinotegana,
cambiando tiros por tragos
y aconsejando a sus muchachas para sacarle información
                    a los marines y guardias.
Directora de correos y espionaje en la región
y hasta ayudaba económicamente.
                    Quién puede decir algo de ella
y de sus putas, las más dignas y limpias que se han
          conocido.

                    Cómo no recordar a la Tiburcia García Otero,
pozo aterrado, hacienda desolada, destazada, encarcelada
y vapuleada en la penitenciaría de Managua
por órdenes expresas del propio Moncada
para que dijera lo que sabía de mí;
pero yo para ella era como otro de sus hijos,
y apenas salió libre voló a estas montañas
          como lora feliz, como chocoya parlera
a hacer de cocinera, de enfermera, de lavandera en el
          ejército.

          Y qué decir de la Bertita Munguía,
                    dirigente obrera,
que organizó protestas ante el traidor de Díaz
y ante el Gobierno de los Estados Unidos . . .

Who could fail to recall
Juana Cruz, Jinotegan bartender,
exchanging brandy for bullets
and advising her girls to extract information
                              from guards and marines.
Director of regional mail and espionage
she even helped out with money.
                    Who could say a word against her
and her whores, the cleanest and most dignified ever
          known.

                    Who could forget Tiburcia García Otero,
her demolished well and desolate ranch; cut up, jailed
and flogged in the Managua penitentiary
by express orders of Moncada himself
to make her tell what she knew about me;
but to her, I was one of her children
and no sooner was she freed than she flew to these
          mountains
like a happy parrot, a loquacious *chocoya*,
to become an army cook, nurse and launderer.

          And there's so much to say about Bertita Munguía,
                    labor leader,
who organized protests against the traitor Díaz
and against the United States government . . .

Y así podría mencionar a tantas y tantas
mujeres
que nos han seguido montaña adentro;
soldados que se juegan la vida y a veces, la pierden.
Guardadoras de secreto donde los hombres son vulnerables
Sus ropas íntimas escondieron mensajes más amorosos
que el amor que nunca conocieron.
Señoras y señoritas de antiguas familias de Managua,
León, Matagalpa y Chinandega
que prestaron efectivos servicios.
Todas ellas montaron dos emboscadas:
El Embocadero y El Bramadero.

Una niña culta y rica es la jefa de Matagalpa.
Muy conservadora y absolutamente insospechable.
Dos jóvenes y una viuda de abolengo de León;
esposas de terratenientes chinandeganos
y hasta la mujer de un Ministro de Moncada
son nuestras.

Cómo no recordar o mencionar a todas nuestras mujeres.
Sin ellas la guerra hubiera sido imposible,
columna invisible de mi ejército;
ellas han tendido el amor entre emboscada y emboscada
y se han tendido al amor con los muchachos.

I could go on naming so many, many
women
who have followed us deep into the mountains;
soldiers who gamble their lives and sometimes lose.
Keepers of secrets where men are vulnerable
Their intimate garments hid messages more loving
than the love they never knew.
Old and young women from the fine families of Managua,
León, Matagalpa and Chinandega
who gave real service.
They all mounted two ambushes:
El Embocadero and El Bramadero.

A rich and cultivated girl is the leader in Matagalpa.
Very conservative and absolutely above suspicion.
Two youths and a widow of León lineage;
wives of Chinandegan landowners
and even the wife of one of Moncada's ministers
are ours.

Who could forget any of our women.
Without them, the war would have been impossible,
my army's invisible column;
they have spread love between ambushes
and extended their love to the boys.

Ni un libro entero bastaría para contar sus acciones
ni todas las estrellas de este cielo scoviano bastaría
                              para compararlas,
pero el viento de esta tierra sabe sus nombres, repite
                              sus nombres,
dice sus nombres mientras pulsa los pinares como si
                              rasgara una honda y oscura guitarra.

No single book would suffice to recount their deeds
nor would all the stars in this Segovian sky suffice
                    for comparison,
but the wind of this earth knows their names, echoes
                    their names,
speaks their names, while it plays the pine groves as if
                    strumming a deep dark guitar.

(MP/BP)

PIE DE FOTO

Con qué gozo recuesta el poeta Julio Valle-Castillo
su cabeza sobre la sien izquierda de Ione Medeiros.
El esplendor de su sonrisa es mayor
que el de su rubia y larga cabellera lacia,
que el de su piel dorada y su cotona amarilla
contrastando con el pelo oscuro y la barba de Julio.

Un árbol de guayaba les da a sus rostros
matices de intimidad y sombra
(la mano abierta del poeta sobre el hombro derecho
       apenas le forma pliegues y roza su pelo).
De fondo, el cielo
       la tapia gris,
         otros bebedores en su mesa
           y difusas trinitarias.

En la foto no aparece el mantel a cuadros,
ni las botellas de Ron Plata,
ni los titiles en salsa que le encantan . . .
ni el lomo relleno, la ensalada de aguacates
y las tajadas tritas con queso.

Ni aparece el otro Julio

PHOTO CAPTION

With pure pleasure the poet Julio Valle-Castillo leans
his head on the left temple of Ione Medeiros.
His smile is more magnificent than her long blond hair,
than her golden skin and yellow blouse
contrasting with his dark hair and beard.

A guayaba tree lends their faces
nuances of intimacy and shadow
(the poet's hand open on her right shoulder scarcely makes
        a crease
and brushes against her hair)
In the background, the sky
        a gray wall,
            other drinkers at a table,
                and blurred bougainvillea.

The checked tablecloth doesn't appear in the photo
nor the bottles of Plata rum
nor the chicken livers in sauce that enchant him . . .
nor the stuffed pork loin, the avocado salad,
the fried bananas with cheese.

Nor does the other Julio appear

único y eficaz mesero de El Mango,
tan chavalo y alegre,
quien fue movilizado a combatir al Sur
y regresó mayor, adusto y reflexivo.

Ni sale la Antonina, ni los chocoyos
que desde arriba del palo casi la cagan;
ni Oscar-René
       ni la China,
ni la Mercha y sus fabulosos cuentos;
       ni tu mano
que bajo la mesa buscaba la mía.
Ni aparezco yo, ni lo feliz que fui
de estar con él y junto a todos ustedes
ese día de Agosto.

Ni el tremendo aguacero que nos remojó más tarde
      menos dichoso
           de lo dichosos que fuimos después.

the lone, efficient waiter in El Mango,
so young and cheerful,
who was mobilized to fight at the Southern Front
and came back older, austere, and thoughtful.

Nor is Antonina there, not the parakeets
on the pole up above that almost shit on her
nor Oscar-René,
        nor La China
nor La Mercha and her fabulous stories,
        nor your hand
that under the table sought mine.
Nor do I appear, nor my happiness
to be with him and with all of you
that day in August.

Nor the tremendous downpour that drenched us later,
        less fortunate
                than we've been since.

DE REGRESO A MÉXICO, D. F.

a Julio Valle-Castillo

Tu ciudad de diez años de estudiante
te traiciona.
Ya no te reconocés en ella, ya no te sirve
más que para la nostalgia.

Te das de frente con todos los muertos:
Herminio Ahumada, viejo combatiente del Vasconcelismo,
sandinista encabronado
íntimo de Pellicer;
un poeta.

Irma Krautz, divorciada,
tan sufrida y tequilera,
eterna enamorada del poeta Cardenal.
— Una linda mujer como un ámbar con una hoja seca
          dentro —

Luis Rius nunca llegó al Festival de Poesía de Michoacán;
se lo llevó el cáncer sin el Nóbel, a los 53 años.

BACK IN MEXICO CITY

For Julio Valle-Castillo

Your city for ten student years
betrays you.
You no longer see yourself in it,
it's now only good for nostalgia.

You come face to face with all the dead:
Herminio Ahumada, old fighter for Vasconcelismo,
ardent Sandinista,
intimate of Pellicer;
poet.

Irma Krautz, divorced,
long-suffering and alcoholic,
forever in love with the poet Cardenal.
— A lovely woman, like amber with a dry leaf inside —

Luis Rius never made it to the Poetry Festival of Michoacán:
he died of cancer at 53, without the Nobel Prize.

José Luis Benítez de tu misma edad,
murió de alcoholismo
al igual que don Ramón Martínez Ocaranza
(el Coronel Urtecho de Morelia).

Si no todos los muertos eran poetas,
eran como de la familia.

Sólo Ernesto Mejía-Sánchez, tu padre y maestro
(que reconoció bajo tus gafas las mancuernillas
de ámbar de don Laureano Castillo)
ha quedado como última y frágil evidencia
del sueño.

Jose Luis Benítez, your age,
died of alcoholism
just like don Ramón Martínez Ocaranza
(the Coronel Urtecho of Morelia).

Though not all the dead were poets,
they were all part of the family.

Only Ernesto Mejía-Sánchez, your father and teacher
(who with your glasses recognized don Laureano Castilo's
amber cufflinks)
has remained as the final, fragile proof
of the dream.

50 VERSOS DE AMOR
Y UNA CONFESIÓN NO REALIZADA
A ERNESTO CARDENAL

De haber conocido a Ernesto como aparece
en una foto amarillenta que Julio me mostró:
flaco, barbón, camisa a cuadros y pantalón de lino,
las manos en los bolsillos y un aire general de desamparo;
me hubiera metido por él en la Rebelión de Abril.
Juntos, habríamos ido a espiar a Somoza
en la fiesta de la embajada yanki.

¿Quién sería su novia en esos días?
La Meche o la Adelita o tal vez Claudia,
Ileana o Myriam. Muchachas eternamente frescas
que sonríen desde viejas fotografías
traspapeladas en quién sabe qué gavetas.

Myriam, sale de la iglesia con su vestido amarillo
entallándole el cuerpo moreno y grácil.
Ileana pasa distante
más lejana que la galaxia de Andrómeda;
la Adelita palidece al doblar la esquina
y encontrarse de pronto con él;
Claudia prefiere las fiestas y las carreras de caballos

50 VERSES OF LOVE
AND AN UNTOLD CONFESSION
FOR ERNESTO CARDENAL

To have known Ernesto as he appears
in a yellowish photograph that Julio showed me:
thin, bearded, checked shirt and linen pants.
his hands in his pockets, and a general air of helplessness;
for him I would have joined the April Rebellion.
Together, we would have spied on Somoza
at the Yankee embassy's party.

Who would have been his girlfriend in those days?
Meche or Adelita or perhaps Claudia,
Ileana or Myriam. Girls forever fresh,
who smile from old photographs
mislaid in who-knows-which drawers.

Myriam, emerges from church, her yellow dress
tailored to her dark, slim body.
Ileana passes distant
more remote than the Andromeda galaxy;
Adelita pales upon turning the corner
and suddenly finding herself with him;
Claudia prefers parties and horse races

a un epigrama de Ernesto.
Meche es la más misteriosa.

Conocí a Ernesto en el año 72, oficiando
en el altar de la ermita de Solentiname.
Ni me habló; apenas me concedió el perfil.
Es la fecha y no se acuerda siquiera
de haberme visto entonces.

Después de la Insurrección del 78 al fin reparó en mí.
Se apareció en la clandestina Radio Sandino
interesado en conocerme al saber que yo era poeta
        y combatiente.
Ni en mis sueños más fantásticos imaginé
que el encuentro sucedería así:
Allí venía tranquilo, como que si nada,
caminando entre el monte recién llovido.
Entró al caramanchel y preguntó por mí.

¿Para qué preguntó? Ese encuentro fue decisivo.
Desde el principio me entendí con él casi tan bien
como en otros tiempos con mi abuelo.
Allí es que comienza una larga historia:
Cuatro años ayudándole a inventar el mundo;
organizando el Ministerio de Cultura
con el fervor y la fe de un niño

to an epigram by Ernesto.
Meche is the most mysterious.

I met Ernesto in 1972, officiating
at the hermitage altar in Solentiname.
He didn't speak to me, barely gave me a glance.
Today is the date and he doesn't remember
having even seen me back then.

After the insurrection of '78 he finally noticed me.
He appeared at clandestine Radio Sandino
interested in meeting me when he learned I was a poet
        and combatant.
Not even in my wildest dreams did I imagine
our encounter would happen like that:
He walked calmly, as though it were nothing at all,
along the hillside wet from recent rain.
He entered the station and asked for me.

Why did he ask for me? That encounter was decisive.
From the beginning I understood him almost as well
as I did my grandfather in other times.
Thus began our long history:
Four years helping him invent the world;
organizing the Ministry of Culture
with the faith and fervor of a child

en la madrugada de su Primera Comunión.
Esos años fueron casi felices (como diría Mejía-Sánchez)

Aunque a estas alturas
        lo conmueva todavía algún recuerdo,
usted jamás se conformó con ninguna:
ni con Claudia, ni con todas las otras que no menciono.
Como San Juan de la Cruz o Santa Teresita (no quería una
        muñeca
sino todas las muñecas del mundo)
sólo estuvo conforme cuando poseyó todo, todito el Amor.

Ahora posee a Dios a través del pueblo: ¡Esposo de Dios!
Por eso cuando le digo que de haber sido yo su novia
en ese entonces sus versos para mí
        no habrían sido en vano,
él me contesta: "qué lástima, no nos ayudó el tiempo";
        pero yo ni caso le hago.

the morning of his First Communion.
Those years were almost happy (as Mejía Sanchez would
                                                                    say)

Even though at this point
            some memory may still stir you
you weren't satisfied with anyone;
not Claudia, not any of the others I don't mention.
Like Saint John of the Cross or Saint Teresa (you didn't want
            one doll
but all the dolls in the world)
you were only satisfied when you possessed it all, all the
                                                                    Love.

Now he possesses God through the people: God's husband!
That's why when I tell him
had I been his girlfriend in those days
his verses for me
            would not have been in vain,
he responds: "What a shame, time wasn't on our side":
            but I don't pay him any mind.

(MP/BP)

ERA UNA ESCUADRA DESPERDIGADA
(Septiembre de 78)

Nadie quería cruzar aquel campo quemado.
(Las cenizas plateadas y algún destello rojo
                    de las últimas brasas).
Te tiraste de primero y tu cuerpo se miraba oscuro
                    contra lo blanco.
Escondidos en el monte los demás esperábamos verte
                    alcanzar la orilla
para irnos cruzando.

Como en cámara lenta lo recuerdo:
el terreno inclinado, resbaloso, caliente
la mano agarrada al fusil
                    el olor a quemado.
El ruido de las hélices
de vez en cuando, ráfagas.

Tus botas se enterraban en lo blando
y levantabas un vaho blanquecino
                    a cada paso.
(Debe haber sido un tiempo
        que se nos hizo largo)

A SCATTERED SQUAD
(September 1978)

No one wanted to cross that burned field.
(Silvery ashes and a red glimmer
                    of the last embers).
You jumped out first and your body looked dark
                    against the white.
Hidden in the forest the rest of us waited to see you
                    reach the edge
before we started to cross.

I remember it like a slow motion film:
the sloping terrain, hot and slippery
your hand grasping your gun
                    the stench of burning.
The sound of propellers
and from time to time, machine guns.

Your boots sank in the softness
and you let out a whitish breath
                    with each step.
(Time must have
        dragged for us)

Todos los compañeros, Dionisio, te mirábamos
nuestros pechos latiendo inútilmente
        bajo la luna llena.

We all watched you, Dionisio,
our hearts beating vainly
        beneath the full moon.

Y MALDIJE LA LUNA
(Septiembre 78)

Hubo una especie de tregua: no se oían disparos.
Empezamos de nuevo a gritar nuestros números
y nos fuimos reuniendo en un terreno
                    pequeño y quebrado.

Creímos ser los únicos sobrevivientes
y deliberamos qué íbamos a hacer:
                    lo único posible
era buscar cómo unirnos
                    a las escuadras de San Judas.

Intentamos irnos por unos montes atrás;
el camino era muy inclinado y dificultoso.
Nos acercamos a unas viviendas
pero unos perros
nos olfateaban como a un kilómetro de distancia
y cada vez que queríamos movernos
                    se ponían como locos.

Tuvimos que quedarnos quietos toda la noche.
Había una luna bellísima, y por primera vez
                    maldije la luna.

AND I CURSED THE MOON
(September 78)

A lull: shots were no longer heard.
We began to call out our numbers
and come back together
       in a small rocky field.

We thought we were the sole survivors
and we discussed what we should do:
          our only option
was to find a way to join
          the squads at San Judas

We tried leaving through the mountains:
a steep and difficult path.
We neared some dwellings
but dogs smelled us a kilometer away;
every time we tried to move
        they went crazy.

All night we had to stay still.
The moon was gorgeous, and for the first time
       I cursed the moon.

REPORTAJE DE LA PROTESTA FRENTE A LA
EMBAJADA DE ESTADOS UNIDOS POR LAS
MANIOBRAS *PINO GRANDE*

¿QUÉ DIJO LEONEL RUGAMA?
                    ¡QUE SE RINDA TU MADRE!
¿Y POR QUÉ?
          PORQUE LA SOBERANÍA DE UN PUEBLO
                    NO SE DISCUTE,
          SE DEFIENDE CON LAS ARMAS EN LA MANO.

Frente a la estatua de Montoya,
viniendo de todas las calles de Managua,
el sol de la tarde nos pega en las caras,
mientras avanzamos
                    avanzamos
                    PUEBLO ÚNETE
                              hacia la embajada.

Por la carretera, bordeada de chilamates,
adelante miles y miles de compañeros,
atrás, miles y miles más;
y al vaivén de las cabezas,
cienes de pancartas, como olas.

A REPORT ON THE PROTEST IN FRONT OF
THE UNITED STATES EMBASSY BY THE
PINO GRANDE MOVEMENT

WHAT DID LEONEL RUGAMA SAY?
            LET YOUR MOTHER SURRENDER!
AND WHY?
        BECAUSE THE SOVEREIGNTY OF A PEOPLE
        IS INDISPUTABLE.
        IT'S DEFENDED WITH WEAPONS IN HAND.

In front of the statue of Montoya,
from all streets in Managua,
we're hit in the face by the afternoon sun,
while we advance
        advance
            PEOPLE UNITED
                toward the embassy.

On the highway, bordered by *chilamate* trees,
thousands and thousands of people in front,
thousands and thousands more behind;
and moving with the heads,
hundreds of signs, like waves.

ESTA ES MI TIERRA
       ESTA ES MI AGUA
NINGÚN YANKI HIJUEPUTA
       PISARÁ A NICARAGUA.

Frente a la embajada queman al Tío Sam.
El embajador Quainton ordena cerrar
              las altísimas verjas.

Primero hablaron las madres de los mártires.
Entre la humazón, sus gritos y lamentos.
Dorados por el polvasal, todos gritamos.
Frente a las verjas herméticas
       gritamos
              gritamos cansados y sedientos.
       Gritamos
              hasta dispersarnos al anochecer.

                    THIS IS MY LAND
                         THIS IS MY WATER
                    NO YANKEE SON-OF-A-BITCH
                              WILL SET FOOT IN NICARAGUA

In front of the embassy they burn Uncle Sam.
Ambassador Quainton orders
            that the highest grates be closed.

First the mothers of martyrs speak.
Amid the dense smoke, their cries and laments.
Gilded by dust, we all cry out.
In front of the hermetic grates
        we cry out
                tired and thirsty we cry out
        We cry out
                until at nightfall we disperse.

EL VENDEDOR DE COCOS

De la fila de acracias junto al adoquinado
el hombre siempre escoge la misma sombra.

Cada día es el rito vaciar el carretón,
separar los cocos, y al filo del machete
ir pelando cada coco hasta dejar
la blanca esfera de carne descubierta.
La mujer los ofrece
            de dos en dos o tres en cada brazo,
sorteando buses,
saltando entre motocicletas y taxis;
pendiente del semáforo
para pegar carrera a recoger más cocos.

Desde lejos, la blancura de los cocos brilla
como los cráneos de los setenta y cinco niños mískitos
muertos por la guardia somocista en Ayapal:

WAN LUHPIA AL KRA NANI BA TI KAIA SA
(Muerte a los asesinos de nuestros hijos)
gritaban sus madres.

Los hijos del vendedor de cocos

THE COCONUT VENDOR

From the row of acacias beside the pavement
the man always picks the same spot of shade.

Every day the same ritual: empty the cart,
separate the coconuts, and with the blade of a machete
begin pealing each coconut until
the white circle of flesh appears.
The woman offers them
            two or three in each arm,
dodging buses,
leaping between motorcycles and taxis;
waiting for the traffic light
to run the gauntlet and get more coconuts.

From afar, the whiteness of the coconuts shines
like the skulls of the seventy-five Miskito children
killed by Somoza's guard in Ayapal:

WAN LUHPIA AL KRA NANI BA TI KAIA SA
(Death to the assassins of our children)
their mothers cry.

The coconut vendor's children

desayunan un coco en la mañana
y almuerzan un coco a medio día
bajo la acacia circundada de cáscaras.

TAWAN ASLA TAKS, TAWAN ASLA TAKS,
(PUEBLO ÚNETE, PUEBLO ÚNETE)
GRITABAN LAS MADRES,
BAILA WALA WINA, BALAYA APIA
BAILA WALA WINA, BALAYA APIA
BAILA WALA WINA, BALAYA APIA
(DEL OTRO LADO, NO PASARÁN).

eat a coconut for breakfast in the morning
and a coconut for lunch at noon
beneath the acacia surrounded by husks.

TAWAN ASLA TAKS, TAWAN ASLA TAKS,
(PEOPLE UNITE, PEOPLE UNITE)
SHOUT THE MOTHERS.
BAILA WALA WINA, BALAYA APIA
BAILA WALA WINA, BALAYA APIA
BAILA WALA WINA, BALAYA APIA
(FROM THE OTHER SIDE, THEY SHALL NOT PASS).

EL VENDE PERIÓDICOS

"CERO POLIOMIELITIS
134,000 MANZANAS ENTREGADAS A LOS CAMPESINOS
15,600 TERRENOS Y VIVIENDAS PARA LOS POBRES
52,000 FAMILIAS RECIBIERON AGUA POTABLE
13,000 MÁS ADQUIEREN ENERGÍA
DEVOLVERÁN A MÍSKITOS Y SUMOS TIERRA USURPADA
        EN EL PASADO"

Ya noche
        bajo los semáforos
                        su cara amarilla
roja, verde
        y otra vez amarilla:

"MILES SE INTEGRAN A LOS CORTES DE CAFÉ
MIL SOMOCISTAS ATACAN DESDE HONDURAS
SANGRE DE SETENTA Y CINCO NIÑOS DERRAMADA EN
                LA MONTAÑA
AL LADO DE LOS COMBATES CONTINUARON LOS
                CORTES DE CAFÉ"

Con su paquete plástico que envuelve
los últimos periódicos del día

THE NEWSBOY

"NO MORE POLIO
134,000 APARTMENT BLOCKS GIVEN TO FARMERS
15,600 PLOTS OF LAND AND HOUSES FOR THE POOR
52,000 FAMILIES GET POTABLE WATER
13,000 MORE GET ELECTRICITY
LAND WILL BE RETURNED TO MISKITOS AND SUMOS"

Night
        beneath the traffic lights
                        his face yellow
red, green
            and yellow again:

"THOUSANDS JOIN THE COFFEE HARVEST
A THOUSAND SOMOCISTAS ATTACK FROM HONDURAS
THE BLOOD OF 75 CHILDREN SPILLED IN THE
                        MOUNTAINS
CLOSE TO THE FIGHTING THE COFFEE HARVEST
                        CONTINUES"

With his plastic package that holds
the day's final editions

                y su camisa
como una vela ondeando
                sobre lo flaquito de su cuerpo:

"QUE CESEN LAS AGRESIONES DESDE TERRITORIO
                HONDUREÑO
18 HERMANOS DEL E.P.S. HAN CAÍDO EN LA ZONA
NORTE NACIONALIZADA LA DISTRIBUCIÓN DEL JABÓN,
                ACEITE Y HARINA.
INQUILINOS TENDRÁN CASA PROPIA
A INSCRIBIRSE EN LOS BATALLONES DE ALGODÓN
CORTES DE CAFÉ, UN TRIUNFO DEL PUEBLO"

Ángel pobre
anunciador de la Historia
                con ojos brillantes del desvelo:

"A SECARSE LAS LÁGRIMAS PARA AFINAR LA PUNTERÍA
SE HARÁ JUSTICIA
                Y SERÁ DEFINITIVA."

                    and his shirt
fluttering like a sail
                    on his thin body:

"END ATTACKS FROM HONDURAN TERRITORY
18 BROTHERS FROM THE E.P.S. HAVE FALLEN IN THE
        NORTHERN ZONE
DISTRIBUTION OF SOAP, OIL AND FLOUR NATIONALIZED
RENTERS WILL HAVE THEIR OWN HOMES
SIGN UP FOR THE COTTON BATTALIONS
COFFEE HARVEST, A TRIUMPH FOR THE PEOPLE

Poor angel,
announcer of History
            his eyes bright with devotion:

"DRY YOUR TEARS TO REFINE YOUR AIM
THERE WILL BE JUSTICE
            AND IT WILL BE DEFINITIVE."

Allen, Roberta. AMAZON DREAM
Angulo de, Jaime. INDIANS IN OVERALLS
Angulo de, G. & J. JAIME IN TAOS
Artaud, Antonin. ARTAUD ANTHOLOGY
Bataille, Georges. EROTISM: Death and Sensuality
Bataille, Georges. THE IMPOSSIBLE
Bataille, Georges. STORY OF THE EYE
Bataille, Georges. THE TEARS OF EROS
Baudelaire, Charles. INTIMATE JOURNALS
Baudelaire, Charles. TWENTY PROSE POEMS
Bowles, Paul. A HUNDRED CAMELS IN THE COURTYARD
Broughton, James. MAKING LIGHT OF IT
Brown, Rebecca. THE TERRIBLE GIRLS
Bukowski, Charles. THE MOST BEAUTIFUL WOMAN IN TOWN
Bukowski, Charles. NOTES OF A DIRTY OLD MAN
Bukowski, Charles. TALES OF ORDINARY MADNESS
Burroughs, William S. THE BURROUGHS FILE
Burroughs, William S. THE YAGE LETTERS
Cassady, Neal. THE FIRST THIRD
Choukri, Mohamed. FOR BREAD ALONE
CITY LIGHTS REVIEW #1: Politics and Poetry
CITY LIGHTS REVIEW #2: AIDS & the Arts
CITY LIGHTS REVIEW #3: Media and Propaganda
CITY LIGHTS REVIEW #4: Literature / Politics / Ecology
Cocteau, Jean. THE WHITE BOOK (LE LIVRE BLANC)
Codrescu, Andrei, ed. EXQUISITE CORPSE READER
Cornford, Adam. ANIMATIONS
Corso, Gregory. GASOLINE
Daumal, René. THE POWERS OF THE WORD
David-Neel, Alexandra. SECRET ORAL TEACHINGS IN TIBETAN BUD-
DHIST SECTS
Deleuze, Gilles. SPINOZA: Practical Philosophy
Dick, Leslie. WITHOUT FALLING
di Prima, Diane. PIECES OF A SONG: Selected Poems
Doolittle, Hilda (H.D.) NOTES ON THOUGHT & VISION
Ducornet, Rikki. ENTERING FIRE
Duras, Marguerite. DURAS BY DURAS
Eidus, Janice. VITO LOVES GERALDINE

Mrabet, Mohammed. THE BOY WHO SET THE FIRE
Mrabet, Mohammed. THE LEMON
Mrabet, Mohammed. LOVE WITH A FEW HAIRS
Mrabet, Mohammed. M'HASHISH
Murguía, A. & B. Paschke, eds. VOLCAN: Poems from Central America
Murillo, Rosario. ANGEL IN THE DELUGE
Paschke, B. & D. Volpendesta, eds. CLAMOR OF INNOCENCE
Pasolini, Pier Paolo. ROMAN POEMS
Pessoa, Fernando. ALWAYS ASTONISHED
Peters, Nancy J., ed. WAR AFTER WAR (City Lights Review #5)
Poe, Edgar Allan. THE UNKNOWN POE
Porta, Antonio. KISSES FROM ANOTHER DREAM
Prévert, Jacques. PAROLES
Purdy, James. THE CANDLES OF YOUR EYES
Purdy, James. IN A SHALLOW GRAVE
Purdy, James. GARMENTS THE LIVING WEAR
Rachlin, Nahid. VEILS: SHORT STORIES
Rey Rosa, Rodrigo. THE BEGGAR'S KNIFE
Rey Rosa, Rodrigo. DUST ON HER TONGUE
Rigaud, Milo. SECRETS OF VOODOO
Ruy Sánchez, Alberto. MOGADOR
Saadawi El, Nawal. MEMOIRS OF A WOMAN DOCTOR
Sawyer-Lauçanno, Christopher, tr. THE DESTRUCTION OF THE JAGUAR
Sclauzero, Mariarosa. MARLENE
Serge, Victor. RESISTANCE
Shepard, Sam. MOTEL CHRONICLES
Shepard, Sam. FOOL FOR LOVE & THE SAD LAMENT OF PECOS BILL
Smith, Michael. IT A COME
Snyder, Gary. THE OLD WAYS
Solnit, Rebecca. SECRET EXHIBITION: Six California Artists
Sussler, Betsy, ed. BOMB: INTERVIEWS
Takahashi, Mutsuo. SLEEPING SINNING FALLING
Turyn, Anne, ed. TOP TOP STORIES
Tutuola, Amos. FEATHER WOMAN OF THE JUNGLE
Tutuola, Amos. SIMBI & THE SATYR OF THE DARK JUNGLE
Valaoritis, Nanos. MY AFTERLIFE GUARANTEED
Wilson, Colin. POETRY AND MYSTICISM
Zamora, Daisy. RIVERBED OF MEMORY